I0148733

Anonymous

A Memorial to Congress to Secure an Adequate Appropriation

for a Prompt and Thorough Improvement of the Mississippi River

Anonymous

A Memorial to Congress to Secure an Adequate Appropriation
for a Prompt and Thorough Improvement of the Mississippi River

ISBN/EAN: 9783744790505

Printed in Europe, USA, Canada, Australia, Japan

Cover: Foto ©ninafisch / pixelio.de

More available books at **www.hansebooks.com**

A

MEMORIAL TO CONGRESS

TO SECURE

AN ADEQUATE APPROPRIATION

FOR A PROMPT AND THOROUGH

IMPROVEMENT OF THE MISSISSIPPI RIVER

WITH AN APPENDIX BY

SYLVESTER WATERHOUSE,

Of Washington University.

EDITION, 5000 COPIES.

ST. LOUIS:
JOHN J. DALY & CO., PRINTERS, 213 NORTH THIRD STREET.
1877.

The following resolution was adopted by the River Improvement Convention, held at St. Paul, Minn., Oct. 11th and 12th, 1877:

Resolved. That the President of this Convention select an Executive Committee of Nine (together with the President of this Convention) whose duty it shall be to prepare a memorial to Congress, setting forth more in detail the views of this Convention upon the subject. of the improvement of the channel of the Mississippi river; to call future conventions if they deem it expedient to do so; to collect and publish statistics bearing on the subject, for the information of the people and of the Government; and to use all further means to procure early and favorable action upon this subject by Congress.

In accordance with the above resolution, the following gentlemen were appointed members of said Committee:

Hon. J. HAM. DAVIDSON, St. Paul, Minn.
Hon. JOHN HOGAN, St. Louis, Mo.
Hon. M. Y. JOHNSON, Galena, Ills.
Gov. E. O. STANARD, St. Louis, Mo.
Hon. J. B. RICHARDS, Dubuque, Iowa.
Mr. JOHN A. SCUDDER, Pres. Me. Ex., St. Louis.
Hon. J. H. BARBER, Chester, Ills.
Prof. C. J. FORSHEY, New Orleans, La.
Mr. FRED'K SCHULENBURG, St. Louis, Mo.

Hon. JOSEPH BROWN, Chairman.

S. WATERHOUSE, Secretary.

LIBRARY

UNIVERSITY OF

CALIFORNIA.

MEMORIAL.

By S. H.

HONORABLE SENATORS AND REPRESENTATIVES OF THE CONGRESS OF THE UNITED STATES:

On the 11th of October, 1877, a Convention met in the city of St. Paul, Minnesota. It was not a political organization. Its members were practical business men, and met under the pressure of a felt necessity to deliberate upon the commercial interests of the Mississippi valley. Through Boards of Trade, Chambers of Commerce, and other organizations, almost every city from the Balize to St. Paul sent delegations. The representatives of the commercial interests of eighteen states sat in council. The Convention, with an earnest concert of action, resolved to petition Congress to provide adequate means for the deepening of the channel of the Mississippi, and for the removal of every obstruction to navigation from St. Paul to the Balize. It is confidently hoped that an appeal which touches such vital interests, and which is sanctioned by the approval of 12,000,000 of people, will receive the favorable consideration of your honorable body.

The Executive Committee appointed by the St. Paul Convention to prepare a memorial to be presented to

Congress respectfully submit the following reasons in favor of an immediate grant of the desired appropriations:

First. The Mississippi vallèy is entitled to better facilities for the transaction of its enormous business. The prosperity of a population of 20,000,000, occupying an area of 1,200,000 square miles, is greatly dependent upon the condition of the Mississippi river.

Obstructions in the Mississippi impair the usefulness and efficiency of 18,000 miles of river navigation. The following figures exhibit the productiveness and wealth of the Mississippi valley. With the exception of Kansas and Nebraska, whose position renders them naturally tributary to the river, the statistics refer exclusively to the states that border upon the banks of the Mississippi.

Area in square miles 694,500
Population in 1870..12,000,000

PRODUCTS IN 1870.

Wheat, bushels............	131,000,000......	Value......$118,425,000
Corn, "	782,000,000......	" 238,465,000
Oats, "	152,000,000......	" 40,840,000
Barley, "	14,540,000......	" 7,455,000
Rye, "	10,000,000......	" 5,666,000
Potatoes, "	41,626,000......	" 22,928,000
Tobacco, pounds............	220,495,000	" 15,700,000
Cotton, "	942,750,000......	" 113,130,000
Sugar (of La. only), "	190,672,500......	" 11,440,000
Hay, tons............	10,611,000......	" 68,857,000
Milch cows, number,.	3,839,000......	" 91,354,000
Cattle, "	6,100,000......	" 107,340,000
Swine, "	14,990,000......	" 91,000,000
Sheep, "	7,260,000......	" 16,660,000
Horses, "	4,462,000......	" 251,900,000
Mules, "	769,000......	" 50,430,000

These impressive aggregates are only a partial exhibition of the fertility and resources of the Mississippi valley. But these products are mere commodities, and the commerce which exchanges and distributes them represents almost incalculable values. The Government Report upon the Internal Commerce of the United States for 1876 affirms that "probably the total *value* of our internal commerce is at least twenty-five times greater than the value of our foreign commerce." But our international trade now amounts to more than $1,000,000,000 annually. Upon the extremely modest assumption that only one-fifth of these exchanges are made in the states that border upon the Mississippi, then commercial values to the extent of $5,000,000,000 are measurably affected by the stage of water in the Mississippi river. It is indeed true that only a very small part of this vast traffic is ever borne upon the waters of the Mississippi, yet it is important to remember that *the rate by river determines the rate by rail.* It is an excess of caution to limit the benefits of an unobstructed Mississippi to the adjacent states—the advantage would be national. The improvement of the river would reduce the cost of transportation throughout the country. Interests of such transcendent magnitude deserve Congressional protection and promotion.

Second. Practical steamboatmen assure this Committee that, if the Mississippi were free from all impediments, the total saving in the less cost, lighter draught, and greater capacity of boats, in greatly reduced rates of insurance, in the avoidance of costly delays, and in the diminished expenses of running, would be fully one-fourth. With a deepened channel, full freights, and an adequate ocean tonnage, the transportation of wheat from St. Paul to Liverpool, by the Mississippi route, would cost eight or ten cents a bushel less than shipments by way of New York.

It is probable that the economy on the heavy freights which would naturally seek exchange by an unobstructed Mississippi would pay for the proposed improvements in a single year. The permanent deepening of the Mississippi river would attract a large foreign trade, and open a cheap entrance to an immigration that would people our wild lands and develop new sources of public wealth. An enlightened Congress cannot afford to neglect the national economy which an improved Mississippi would insure. The *possible* saving in the movement of our boundless harvests and heavy merchandise is almost inestimable. There is now an urgent demand for retrenchment—but there is no economy which would so greatly enrich the nation as a liberal outlay for the immediate improvement of the Mississippi.

Third. The facilities which an unobstructed Mississippi would afford for national unity and defense cannot wisely be ignored. Material ties are perhaps the strongest alliance of states. The bonds of great and recognized interest are nearly indissoluble. The military service which the Mississippi and its tributaries rendered in the late war was memorably efficient. The foremost governments of Europe long since adopted the policy of effectively improving their rivers. A policy which bears such historic sanctions of wisdom and utility forcibly commends itself to the consideration of American statesmen.

Fourth. In earlier years, our Government did not fully appreciate the importance of the Mississippi valley. In the distribution of Congressional appropriations, a disproportionate share was allotted to the sea-board and the lakes. But latterly there has been a juster recognition of the commercial interests of this valley.

It is earnestly hoped that our Government will not forsake the liberal policy which has lately guided its action. Indeed entire justice to the west would require a still more generous treatment. There is now in the Mississippi valley a preponderance of the population and business of the whole United States.

The Mississippi, which forms the border-line of ten states, and which, within the limits of navigation, has a bank-line of 4000 miles, is too important a factor in the commerce of this country for the Government any longer to permit its efficacy to be diminished by the presence of obstructions.

Fifth. There is an urgent need of an immediate and liberal appropriation for the improvement of the Mississippi river. The speedy completion of this work would not only open a great thoroughfare to national prosperity and enable the country to avail itself of exceptionally favorable conditions for the extension of its foreign trade, but it would also effect an ultimate saving for the Government itself. Occasionally the appropriations have been so inadequate and the intervals between them so long, that before the resumption of the work, the improvements have been entirely swept away, or only preserved in a state of partial completion and utter uselessness.

Gen. J. H. Simpson, of the U. S. Engineers, has under his charge the section of the Mississippi which extends from the mouth of the Illinois to the mouth of the Ohio. In response to inquiries, this officer recently addressed a communication to this Committee, in which he expressed the following views :

" I am satisfied that seven appropriations of $1,000,000 each would accomplish fully as much as twenty of $500,000 each in the prosecution of works of the character required in the Mississippi. If appropriations are to be limited to $200,000, or thereabouts, per year, it would be as well to abandon the expectation of an improved river, for it will never be realized. Such sums would enable many local improvements, of more or less value, to be made, but nothing towards a permanent deep channel."

There are several public improvements of the Mississippi now in progress. In their unfinished state, they are useless and insecure. To prevent an idle expenditure of money, Congress ought at once to appropriate a sufficient sum to complete these works and free the navigation of the Mississippi from every impediment.

In compliance with the instructions of the St. Paul Convention, this Committee asks Congress to grant an appropriation of $2,000,000 for the improvement of the Mississippi, and to authorize the expenditure—under the supervision of Government Engineers—of definite sums upon specific portions of the river, as follows :

Upon the section from St. Paul to the head of Keokuk Rapids...$617,000
  "   "   "   the foot of Keokuk Rapids to the mouth
                          of the Illinois.............. 383,000
  "   "   "   the mouth of the Illinois to Cairo......... 500,000
  "   "   "   Cairo to New Orleans...................... 500,000

The first amount recommended in this special assignment of appropriations accords with the estimate of the

U. S. Engineer who has charge of the upper section of the river.

Your Committee believe that the proposed appropriation is justified by every consideration of public economy and commercial prosperity.

A river endowed with such vast capabilities of usefulness should be fitted for its grand destiny. But the Mississippi can never fulfil its great office of commercial exchange, till it possesses in the lowest stages of water a permanent channel of the following depth:

From St. Paul to St. Louis............................. .... 5 feet
" St. Louis to Cairo... 8 "
" Cairo to New Orleans............................. ....10 "

By a formal vote, the Executive Committee have expressed an earnest desire that " the Government, in addition to appropriations for the improvement of the Mississippi river, will also provide for the removal of obstructions from the channels leading to adjacent ports where custom-houses are located and imposts collected."

In the name, then, of the commercial interests of this valley, we respectfully yet earnestly ask your honorable body to grant the petition of your memorialists, and make an early and adequate appropriation for the improvement of the channel of the Mississippi.

In behalf of the Executive Committee on Mississippi River Improvements,

JOSEPH BROWN,
Chairman.

S. WATERHOUSE,
Secretary.

APPENDIX.

The following paper, prepared in the interest of the St. Louis Board of Trade, was submitted to the St. Paul Convention and referred by that body to its Executive Committee for action. In accordance with a vote of this Committee, the article—enlarged by the introduction of a few statistics which have been obtained since the date of the Convention—is annexed to the memorial, as a fuller presentation of the arguments in favor of a Congressional appropriation.

WASHINGTON UNIVERSITY,

SAINT LOUIS, MO.

Hon. JOSEPH BROWN,

President of the St. Paul River Improvement Convention:

DEAR SIR: Having been honored by the St. Louis Board of Trade with an appointment as one of its delegates to this Convention, I greatly regret that professional duties will prevent my attendance. An enforced absence constrains me to submit my views by letter.

COST OF DETENTIONS.

A recent trip from St. Paul to St. Louis by boat has deeply impressed me with the necessity of improving the Mississippi river. One of my associates sailed from

Moville, a port of northern Ireland, about the same time that I left St. Paul, and he actually reached St. Louis first, making a journey of over 4000 miles in less time than I was able to make a voyage of 800 miles!

In good stages of water, it usually takes a boat four days to go from St. Paul to St. Louis. The round trip of 1600 miles, including stoppages at every point for passengers and freight, has been made in less than seven days. But my return, including two days of waiting for the steamer which had been detained by low water, occupied thirteen days!

Nor is this an isolated case. During the past summer, thousands of passengers have experienced similar, though not perhaps equal, detentions; and thousands of tons of merchandise have been detained, by the low stage of water, for days beyond the proper time of shipment and delivery. In these days of rapid exchanges, nowhere is the truth of the adage that "time is money" more sensibly felt than in the transactions of commerce. The delay of passengers or goods implies loss. In the consumption of coal, in the wages of the crew, in the salaries of the officers, in the interest on vested capital, in the loss of possible profits, and in the interruption of the errands of friendship and commerce, the damage which any protracted detention inflicts upon steamboat companies, upon merchants and passengers, is always serious.

An intelligent steamboat captain, whose judgment has been informed and matured by more than twenty years of service, recently assured me that the cost of the detention of an upper Mississippi steamer was $16 an hour. Upon the assumption that the cost per hour is only one-half of this estimate, then the loss on our trip alone was more than $1300; and the aggregate losses which all of the boats incurred from detention by low water must amount during the present season to an immense sum.

This has been a year of exceptionally low water, but every season there is more or less interruption of navigation by sand-bars, and the total loss is very heavy. In 1867, the Northern Line Packet Companies paid over $200,000 for lightering over the Keokuk Rapids, and during the last six weeks of that season they did not receive more than half the grain that was offered, because it cost so much to transfer it over the rapids. How many hundred thousand dollars the sand-bars have cost the company this year may be inferred from the preceding figures. But the damage from obstructed navigation is an *annual* assessment upon the prosperity of the country, and the loss of any one year, however great, sinks into insignificance when compared with the total losses that have ensued since the first steamboat cleft the waters of the Mississippi.

The benefits of an unobstructed navigation of the Mississippi have become national, but heretofore the injuries of an interrupted navigation have been individual. This is clearly unjust. At a cost of over $4,000,000, the Government has constructed around the Keokuk Rapids a canal eight miles long, three hundred feet wide, and five feet deep. The work is a noble, though tardy, recognition of the material interests of the Mississippi valley. In high water, the canal is unnecessary; and in low water, when it is most needed, its usefulness is greatly impaired by the obstructions above and below it. The presence of five feet of water in the canal is a fact of vastly less commercial importance, if in scores of places in the upper Mississippi there are only two and one-half or three feet of water. It is easy to see how materially the numerous sand-bars which blockade 500 miles of the upper Mississippi restrict the utility of eight miles of uninterrupted navigation. To complete the usefulness of the canal, the Government will be compelled to maintain a channel of equal depth throughout the length of the upper Mississippi.

DISCOURAGEMENT OF AGRICULTURAL INDUSTRY.

According to the judgment of commercial experts, the value of the traffic on the upper Mississippi, is about $400,000,000 a year. The means of verifying this estimate are not at hand. If the statement is only an approximation, it still shows the colossal magnitude of the river trade. Of this grand aggregate, the business experience of the Keokuk Northern Line Packet Company* proves that at least one-half is diverted from river to rail by the vexations and delays arising from shallow water. This diversion generally increases the cost of transportation and diminishes the profits of agriculture. Now it is a sound principle of political economy that the *creators* of wealth should never be subjected to oppressive burdens.

To cities situated on the banks of the Mississippi, the railroads grant river rates, but heavily assess the towns which are not adjacent to the stream. These unjust discriminations exact a burdensome tribute from the farmers. When the water is high, the railroads reduce their charges to the lowest practicable point, in order successfully to compete with the river, but when the water is low, or the river is closed by ice, then the railroads profiting by the

---

*The testimony of this company is emphasized by the magnitude of their commercial operations. Their fleet now consists of sixteen steamers, three tow-boats, and forty-five barges.

embarrassments of an obstructed navigation raise their tariffs, and the difference in the rates comes, partly at least, out of the pockets of the farmers. This unnecessary tax disheartens agricultural industry and represses the production of wealth. When the discouraged farmer finds that, after all his hard work, it costs nearly as much to send his grain to market as he gets for it, he is inclined to restrict his industry to the satisfaction of his domestic wants, and the country loses those possible values which a cheap system of transportation would have stimulated him to produce.

The improvement of the Mississippi river would cheapen breadstuffs throughout the land and confer a mutual benefit upon producer and consumer. The western farmer could save more money and consequently could buy more goods, while the eastern manufacturer could live more cheaply and therefore could sell his fabrics at a lower price. In these times of industrial adversity, a public work that tends to lessen the cost of subsistence is specially worthy of the active encouragement of the Government.

THE RELATIVE CHEAPNESS OF WATER FREIGHTS.

Obviously carriage by water is far cheaper than transportation by rail. *Rival trains* never run on the same railroad, but any number of competitive boats can ply on the same river. Every railway company possesses its own track, but no corporation has an exclusive title to the Mississippi river. Apart from its natural cheapness, river freightage is still further reduced by the active competition of different lines of steamers. Even if the Mississippi were not used for commercial purposes, yet there would be a great economy in improving its channel, for the mere possibility of its use would force the railroads to lower their charges to river rates, and the total saving in the price of transportation would many times exceed the cost of the proposed improvements.

CARRYING CAPACITY OF BARGES.

The heavy expense of construction, equipment, running and repairs, the large force required for their operation, and the comparatively small work accomplished by a single engine, must always render railroads a costly system of transportation. The bounty of Providence has freely provided the river for our commercial convenience. There is no cost of construction, but only of improvement. In a good stage of water, even upon the upper Mississippi, a steam-tug can tow eight or ten barges, and the freight of these barges, if fully loaded, would fill respectively trains of 384 and 480 cars. What a number of engines, force of men, and outlay of money it would take to transfer by rail the load of a single tow-boat! On the lower Mississippi, the achievements of the tow-boats are still more extraordinary. A steam-tug once towed into New Orleans a fleet of barges whose cargo would have freighted 1500 cars! This exceptional exploit shows the possibility of the barge system.

Forty-six coal-fleets were once detained at Pittsburg Landing by low water. Released from their embargo by a sudden rise of the river, 369 coal-flats, bearing a freight of more than 4,000,000 bushels of coal, sailed from the port of Pittsburg within the brief period of three days. In 1876, Pittsburg shipped by river—mostly to towns on the lower Mississippi—more than 62,000,000 bushels of coal. A large portion of this coal was destined for the use of river and ocean steamers—a fact of significant importance in its relation to the foreign trade of the Mississippi valley. The total investments of Pittsburg in coal-transports amount to $5,000,000. These facts, which are authorized by a Government Report, not only exhibit the carrying capacity of barges, but also show the enormous amount of tonnage which its affluents contribute to the commerce of the Mississippi.

During the present season, more than thirty steamboats have been running upon the waters of the upper Missouri and the Yellowstone.

The number and tonnage of all the craft now plying on the Mississippi and its affluents form aggregates which will doubtless surprise persons unfamiliar with the magnitude of our river commerce.

According to the Bureau of Statistics, the gross enrolled tonnage of the Mississippi and its tributaries was as follows:

FISCAL YEAR, 1876.

No. of vessels...2,865

Tons...400,512

Official records justify an addition to this aggregate of 95 vessels and 20,000 tons as the *un*enrolled tonnage of the port of St. Louis alone.

It will aid our conception of the vast amount of merchandise which these fleets can transport to recollect that, during the business season, even the raft-boats make numerous trips; and some of the large steamers, plying on limited courses, make one hundred voyages. If the present commerce of the Mississippi is so enormous, what would be its limit after the channel has been permanently deepened?

2

NATURAL ROUTES OF TRANSIT.

Where there are no obstructions to navigation, bulky commodities instinctively seek water transit.

The foregoing statement has been singularly confirmed by recent changes in the movement of grain. It is estimated by the Government Statistician that "ninety-two per cent. of the freights shipped east from Chicago by lake consists of breadstuffs."

The following figures—which are worthy of a careful examination—all refer to the shipments of wheat from the Mississippi valley to the Atlantic seaboard:

Shipments during the two weeks ending May 12th, 1877:
By rail ....2,550,000 bushels.
By lake 4,490,000   "

Shipments during the two weeks ending October 12th, 1877:
By rail ....1,955,000 bushels.
By lake 9,563,000   "

Shipments *by rail* during the eleven weeks ending
October 14th, 1876..17,893,800 bushels.
    "   "   1877...10,653,100   "

It will be observed that the wheat transported in May was the remnant of the relatively small crop of 1876; but even then, when the quantity of cereal tonnage was less than usual, the amount of wheat carried east *by rail*, was about one-third larger than the shipments by car in the busiest portion of 1877, after a harvest of unparalleled abundance. In view of the extraordinary crop of the present season, it might naturally be supposed that the quantity of wheat conveyed *by rail* would be much larger this year than it was last year; but statistics show that, during eleven weeks only of the present season, there has been a comparative decrease of over 7,000,000 bushels in rail freights. Since the new harvest was garnered, the railroads have carried scarcely one-half of the grain which they had the facilities to handle. Meanwhile the lake and canal boats have been freighted almost to the limit of their capacity. The preceding tables show a surprising increase in transit by the water route. For a given time during the present year, the fall shipments by lake and canal were more than double the spring shipments. The season of transit and the extent of the harvest only partially account for this increase; the full explanation of this larger patronage of the lakes must be sought in the popularity and economy of water carriage. These facts significantly indicate how' vast a commerce would float upon the Mississippi, if its channel were always open to an unobstructed navigation.

With late exceptions, the railroads have for the last fifteen years been steadily gaining business at the expense of the water routes. The friends of the river can cherish no reasonable hope of a successful competition with the railways in the conveyance of express goods and light merchandise. It is chiefly in the foreign exportation of cereals and other heavy wares that a just expectation of a material enlargement of the river trade may be entertained. The reason why so much business has been diverted from the Mississippi is obvious. The existing obstacles have discouraged investments in steamboat property and prevented that full equipment, compact organization, and vigorous co-operation which have achieved such success on the lakes. The uncertainty, delay, and cost incident to a difficult navigation have largely prevented merchants from forwarding their commodities to foreign markets by the Mississippi route; while capitalists have been deterred from establishing lines of steamships to New Orleans by the obstructions at the Balize, and by doubts of their ability to procure full and regular cargoes.

With an improved channel, the Mississippi would bear unfailing supplies of tonnage to Atlantic steamers, and then a largely increased trade, together with an intimate co-operation of river and ocean lines, would permit a still further reduction in the rates of freightage to foreign markets.   •

RELATIVE RATES BY RIVER AND RAIL.

Mercantile experience warrants the assertion that three and one-third mills per ton per mile on cargoes of grain and heavy merchandise transported by river is a paying rate.* But freight cannot be profitably carried on railroads for less than eight and three-fourth mills per ton per mile, and the *average* tariff, even for through consignments, is from one cent to one cent and a half per ton per mile. It is indeed true that the charges have at times been less than these figures, in consequence of the rivalry of different roads, or of the efforts of railways to divert shipments from the Mississippi, but this competition has proved disastrously unprofitable. Perhaps to this unnatural rivalry the bankruptcies of railway companies, and the turbulence and wild disorder which have lately disturbed the industries of the nation may partly owe their origin. Possibly the cause of the inability of the railroads

---

* The above figures are based upon the information of practical steamboatmen. But according to official authority, the statement is an over-estimate of freight charges by river.

"The cost of transportation on the river is but *one* mill per ton per mile, or only about *one-tenth* of the average cost of the tonnage movement on the railroads west of the Mississippi, and only *one-sixth* of the average cost of transportation on the Pennsylvania railroad."—*U. S. Gov. Rep. Int. Com. and Nav.*

to pay their workmen customary wages was an excessive reduction of rates for the purpose of competing with the great water routes. The railways are grandly useful avenues of commerce, but they should not attempt to monopolize the carrying trade of the country. With the revival of industrial prosperity, it will test the capacity of both river and rail to effect our commercial exchanges; and meanwhile the railroads should not endeavor, by a competition whose success will inevitably prove fatal to themselves, to divert bulky commodities from their natural channels of transit. With a uniform stage of deep water, grain can be shipped from St. Paul to Liverpool by way of the Gulf eight or ten cents a bushel cheaper than by any other route.

After the close of navigation, when there is no longer any regulation of freights by river competition, the railroads increase their charges, and then the difference between the summer rate by river and the winter rate by rail becomes materially greater. Multiply the cereal exports of the Mississippi valley by the saving per bushel by the river route, and the product is a startling proof of the economy which water carriage can effect.

ECONOMY IN THE MOVEMENT OF CEREALS.

The extent of this possible saving in freightage is impressively shown by the fact that this year the five states of Minnesota, Wisconsin, Iowa, Illinois and Missouri, will be able to export 100,000,000 bushels of wheat alone! Except in California, my eyes never gazed upon such magnificent prospects of agricultural wealth as I recently saw in the fields of Minnesota. In whatever direction my excursions led, on every side there stretched to the limits of vision broad acres of golden grain. Minnesota alone produces this season more than 30,000,000 bushels of wheat, of which 25,000,000 bushels can be spared for exportation. The wheat crop of the other northwestern states is equally bountiful.

But wheat is only one of the commodities of this valley. In 1876, the corn crop of the states contiguous to the Mississippi, including Kansas and Nebraska, was more than 780,000,000 bushels, and its value was over $238,000,000. From its bulkiness, corn is naturally a water freight. This obvious fact is confirmed by commercial statistics. For the last two years, the shipments of corn from Chicago were as follows:

	1875.	1876.
By lake	21,850,000 bushels.	28,100,000 bushels
By rail	4,321,000 "	17,299,000 "

From these figures it will be seen that, in spite of the desperate competition which the railroads have for the last few years been carrying on with water carriage, the lake route has maintained its ascendency.

The foreign consumption of American maize is rapidly increasing. Our exportations prove that a knowledge of the excellence of Indian corn as a cheap and nutritive food for men and animals is fast spreading throughout Europe.* In 1875, the amount of corn exported from the

---

* The price of corn is usually less than half the market rate of wheat: and, according to the following analysis, the nutritious power of Indian corn is but little inferior to that of the best wheat:

	Fine English Wheaten Flour.	Indian Corn Meal.
Water	16	14
Gluten	10	12
Fat	2	8
Starch, &c	72	66
	100	100

Johnston's Chemistry of Common Life.

United States was a little more than 20,000,000 bushels; in 1876, it was over 50,000,000 bushels; in 1877, it was upwards of 70,000,000 bushels. When the United States Department in the French Exposition has made Europe fully familiar with the rich and healthful qualities of our great staple, then the foreign demand for Indian corn will be greatly enlarged. The capacity of the west to produce maize is practically illimitable. In 1877, the corn crop of the United States was 1,340,000,000 bushels. Though nearly all of this immense yield was grown in the Mississippi valley, still only a small portion of our broad prairies has as yet been brought under cultivation. A single quotation from market rates will show the possible profit of the corn trade. On the 21st of last November, the price of corn in St. Louis was forty-four and one-half cents per bushel, and in Liverpool eighty-seven cents a bushel. At that date, the cost of transportation by way of the Gulf, including transfer and insurance charges, was thirty-one cents per bushel. A profit of eleven and one-half cents per bushel on all the surplus corn of the Mississippi valley would soon restore our olden prosperity.

The lower the cost of water transit, the further farmers could afford to send their products to market. Every reduction in river rates would bring to the Mississippi the tribute of a broader empire, and enlarge its commerce by increasing supplies of freight. The economies of an improved channel, saving ten or possibly fifteen cents a bushel on all grain exported by the Gulf route, would give an immense impulse and expansion to the commerce of this valley.

After the deepening of the channel, the river will possess many advantages over the lake route. From Keokuk to the Balize, the Mississippi is sometimes open to navigation all winter, and in the severest seasons the ice-blockade seldom lasts more than two months. But on the lakes, navigation is usually suspended about four months. At present, most of the grain exported from Chicago is shipped in propellers, but the carrying capacity of even the largest of these boats is greatly inferior to the aggregate tonnage of an ordinary fleet of Mississippi barges. To withstand the violence of storms, the lake barges are large and strongly built. The absence of engines is their chief distinction from propellers. The Mississippi barges, not being exposed to the turbulence of inland seas, admit of a relatively lighter and cheaper construction. The lake barges probably cost two or three times as much as the river barges. The tonnage of a lake barge somewhat exceeds that of a river barge ; but on the lakes a steam-tug can tow only two or three barges, while on the upper Mississippi a steam-tug can tow from six to ten barges, and on the lower Mississippi an almost unlimited number. The current of the lakes is so slight as to be an unfelt element in their navigation, but the current of the Mississippi is an effective force. The rapidity of flow varies from three to five miles an hour. The energy of the current alone almost suffices for motive power. As all the cereal cargoes of the Mississippi are carried *down* stream, the co-operation of the current is an important element in transportation. With all these various sources of economy, the improved Mississippi must be a much cheaper course to foreign markets than the lake route. It is believed that the improvement of the river and organized competition would reduce the freight to Liverpool to twenty-five cents per bushel. Is it not the duty of the Government to open the channel through which so full a tide of wealth would flow?

LUMBER TRADE OF THE UPPER MISSISSIPPI.

Lumber interests of an importance scarcely inferior to that of the grain trade are deeply involved in this scheme of improvement. The total quantity of logs and lumber rafted down the upper Mississippi now reaches an annual average of 1,000,000,000 feet, and represents a value of $15,000,000. Of this amount, about 900,000,000 feet are absorbed by the towns along the river, and 100,000,000 feet are brought to the lumber yards of St. Louis. The lumber which is not consumed by the river towns is sent into the interior by rail. The range of distribution varies from 100 miles east of the Mississippi to 1000 miles west of the river. The lumber business can never be diverted from the Mississippi. Wherever the possibility exists, it will always be done by river. But low water subjects raftsmen to embarrassing and expensive detentions. The necessity of employing larger crews and heavier tow-boats materially increases the costs of navigation. According to the judgment of practical lumbermen, the permanent deepening of the channel of the Mississippi would diminish the expense of rafting by fully one-third of the present rates. The improvement of the river would reduce the price of lumber throughout the Mississippi valley.

By the discharge of its duty, the Government would relieve momentous interests from grave embarrassments, and confer an appreciated favor upon the humble pioneers who are struggling to erect homes of their own in the wilds of the west.

MAGNITUDE OF OTHER COMMODITIES.

Nor does lumber close our inventory of valuable commodities.

During the fiscal year 1876, the United States shipped to Europe more than 550,000,000 pounds of pork and other swine products, and the total value of these consignments was $67,800,000.

During the eighteen months ending March 31st, 1877, over 34,000,000 pounds of fresh beef—worth $3,000,000—were exported from this country. The foreign trade in American uncured beef is rapidly extending. Its cheapness and excellence strongly recommend this food to the nations of Europe. Under the improved processes of chilling, the meat reaches foreign stalls fresh and sound. This trade, now in its infancy, will yet develop into proportions of commanding importance.

But the demands of trans-Atlantic nations cannot exhaust our resources. The Mississippi valley could easily supply all the meat markets of Europe.

The almost measureless abundance of other kinds of produce, the heavy southern staples, and the varied products of our factories and work-shops are all seeking domestic or foreign exchange. An economical movement of these commodities is a subject worthy of the gravest attention of our Government. The shipment to market of our plenteous harvests would revive our languishing industries and bless the land with a renewal of public prosperity. Free from obstructions, the Mississippi could easily and cheaply float these products to market.

The Chief of the Bureau of Statistics, in his Report upon the Internal Commerce and Navigation of the United

States for 1876, asserts that "the *tonnage* transported on the various avenues of internal commerce is more than one hundred times greater than the tonnage composing our foreign commerce."

Of this domestic trade, whose magnitude bewilders the imagination, more than one-half of the exchanges are made in the Mississippi valley; and the Mississippi river, if free from impediments, would be pre-eminently our greatest single factor in the transaction of this enormous business. When the interests involved are so vast . and when the necessities of public relief are so urgent, is it not the imperative duty of our Government promptly to remove from this majestic stream every obstacle to navigation?

In 1867, it was thought that the completion of the Keokuk canal would effectually open the navigation of the Mississippi river; but subsequent years of unusually low water render further action necessary. And now the same arguments which advocated the construction of that great work plead for the improvement of the channel of the upper Mississippi. While the obstructions remain, the annual loss in costly delays, in interest on capital, in local decrease of production, in higher tariffs of transit, and in exorbitant rates of insurance, would more than pay for the projected improvements.

GRANTS OF LAND AND CREDIT TO RAILROADS.

Our Government wisely assisted in building the Union Pacific Railroad, and that road, in spite of the mistakes and frauds which have been committed, has proved a national benefit. And I profoundly believe that sound policy will justify our Government, under safeguards that will defy any spoliation of our National Treasury, in granting the loan of its credit to the Northern and Southern Pacific Railways. In the settlement of new lands, in the development of natural resources, in the increase of taxable property, in the additional employment and products of labor, the accession to the public wealth would far exceed the expenditures upon the work. But why should our Government lavish $100,000,000* upon the construction of railroads, and yet hesitate to give half a dozen millions for the improvement of our rivers?

APPROPRIATIONS FOR HARBORS AND LIGHT-HOUSES.

The many millions which the Government has spent upon the harbors and light-houses of the sea-board were judicious outlays for the protection of life and the encouragement of international trade. But our total foreign commerce—which now amounts to about $1,100,000,000 a year—is less than the annual traffic upon the Mississippi and its tributaries. Is our foreign trade alone worthy of the fostering care of the Government? Discontinue our foreign commerce, and the essential comforts of the American people would scarcely be diminished; but suspend our river navigation, and there is not a working-man in the land who would not feel, in the higher cost of living, this interruption of cheap exchange. The ocean conveys to our shores the costly luxuries which embellish the residences of the rich; the river brings to the humble homes of the poor a cheaper means of livelihood. Which deserves the first consideration of our Government? There can be

---

*Up to January 1st, 1877, the extent of Government land-grants to the railroads of the United States was over 200,000,000 acres, and the aid in bonds and accrued interest amounted to more than $90,000,000.

no valid objection to the improvement of our seaports, but the rivers of the Mississippi valley are entitled to equal commercial facilities. The aid which has justly been granted in the one instance cannot rightfully be withheld in the other.

DOMESTIC POLICY OF FOREIGN NATIONS.

The imperial powers of Europe have long favored the policy of internal improvements. France especially has derived from its public works large dividends of material prosperity and social well-being. The vast system of improvements which England has constructed in India has not only preserved its eastern empire, but has also conferred benefits and inaugurated reforms which the administration could not otherwise have accomplished. Without these works, the ghastly tragedy of starvation which has lately been enacted in that unhappy land would have been incalculably more destructive. England has already spent some $500,000,000 upon the railways and other public improvements of India, and British statesmen are now urging their Government, with fair probabilities of success, to expend $150,000,000 more in the construction of works of irrigation so vast as to insure ample harvests and prevent the recurrence of famine.

A policy that has always proved so beneficial abroad cannot be unworthy of adoption by our own Government.

INCREASE OF IMMIGRATION.

There are many reasons of a general character why Congress should take immediate action. The river should be ready for the enormous commerce which will soon float upon its waters. The signs of this early expansion of trade are numerous. Into the broad and fertile tract of land lying immediately east of the Rocky Mountains and stretching from Mexico to the British possessions, tens of thousands of settlers are now pouring. For many months the cars of the Northern Pacific Railroad have been filled with a steady stream of immigrants, and the freight trains have been heavily loaded with their household furniture and farming implements. On the other roads further south, the western trains have also been thronged with immigrants. And when the magnitude of this year's harvest has been published to the world, the magnificent advertisement will cause still larger numbers to seek these new lands. The region extending 500 or 600 miles northwest of St. Paul is as well adapted to wheat culture as any portion of the Mississippi valley. This new northwest will export 2,000,000 bushels of wheat this very season. The products of the extreme northern section will doubtless seek an outlet by Duluth and the lakes, but from its southern limits to the borders of Mexico, the produce of the newly opened farms will naturally find their way to market by way of the Mississippi river. Unless there is a cheap means of transit, the cost of transportation from such remote localities would exceed the profits of production. The inexpensive freightage which the improved channel of the Mississippi would afford will enable these farmers profitably to ship their surplus products to market. The river should be seasonably prepared for the additional business which it will soon be required to transact.

FOREIGN TRADE OF SOUTH AMERICA.

From the domestic traffic of the Mississippi river, there is a natural transition to its foreign exchanges. Prominent among the countries with which the west could carry on a direct and greatly profitable trade, stands South America. The foreign commerce of the South American states is immense. Numerous lines of steamers are steadily pouring the wealth of their rich cargoes into the coffers of the British and French merchants who control this trade. The United Kingdom sends seven or eight steamships a month to South American waters, and there is scarcely a day in the year in which a steamer does not sail from some European port for the same destination. From South America, the voyage to Liverpool is about 3000 or 4000 miles longer than that to New Orleans. The freight on this additional distance is equivalent to a heavy tariff in favor of North American competition. Yet England and France possess almost a monopoly of the foreign trade of South America.

The commerce of Great Britain, France, and the United States with South America, is shown in the following exhibit:

YEAR.	COUNTRY.	EXPORTS.	IMPORTS.
1875	Great Britain	$82,120,000	$105,500,000
"	France	59,724,000	69,179,000
1876	United States	21,600,000	64,588,000

From this table it appears that the profits on a total trade of more than $300,000,000 are now enriching England and France. By an organized and energetic co-operation, a large part of this lucrative business could be diverted to the United States. Nearly one-eighth of all our South American imports come from Brazil, but the balance-sheet of our commerce with our tropical neighbor is a disheartening spectacle to a citizen of the United States. In 1876, our imports from Brazil were $45,453,000, and our exports $7,253,000!

At present, there is comparatively but little intercourse between the twin lands of this continent. In the absence of an American line of steamers, the merchants desirous of exchanging visits and unwilling to encounter the vexatious delay incident to a voyage on a sailing vessel are obliged to make a long and costly detour by way of England.

There are symptoms, however, of an approaching change. The flour, machinery, and furniture of the United States are gradually becoming more popular in the markets of South America. New England, which is now actually sending cotton goods to Manchester and wresting from English manufacturers their long-established supremacy in the markets of China and Japan, will probably in future years supply Brazil and its neighbor states with their *cotton* fabrics. But the Mississippi valley ought now to fill all South American orders for heavy machinery and agricultural products. It is, indeed, surprising that the sagacity and enterprise of the merchants of this valley have not made earlier efforts to secure this enriching trade. A company was recently organized for the purpose of establishing a line of steamers between New Orleans and South American ports. But this undertaking will hardly succeed, unless a sufficient quantity of cheap freight can be obtained at New Orleans; but cheap freight in the Cresent City implies a transportation untaxed with the charges of costly interruptions. Here, then, is another reason of paramount weight for the prompt improvement of the channel of the Mississippi.

IRON INTERESTS OF THE MISSISSIPPI VALLEY.

The physical character of this valley will shape its industrial destiny. Our vast resources of iron and coal foreordain this region to be the great central machine-shop of the nation. St. Louis—now the third city in the United States in manufacturing importance—is already eminent for the excellence of its hardware. The fame of its foundries and work-shops has traversed the ocean and reached distant lands. A large Russian order for machinery was recently filled in this city. These facts have remote bearings, and possibilities of productive results. The British exportation of iron and steel ware to Australia is not one-tenth as large as it was three years ago, while within the same time the Australian demand for American cutlery and hardware has increased twenty fold. Now St. Louis is thousands of miles nearer to the markets of Australia than any eastern or European seat of iron manufactures; and the completion of the Southern Pacific Railroad to San Diego will open a thoroughfare 600 or 800 miles shorter than the present route. Then, with the channel of the Mississippi freed from all obstacles, and with the cheap freights which the competition of an *independent* Southern Pacific Railway would insure, seemingly it would be possible for St. Louis to control the profitable hardware trade of that distant continent.

SIGNS OF RETURNING PROSPERITY.

The skies so long overcast are beginning to show gleams of a brighter day. Already there is an encouraging revival in manufacturing industry. In 1875, the exportation of cotton fabrics from the United States amounted to only $3,000,000; in 1877, it rose to $10,000,000. The Atlantic states do not produce one-tenth part of the breadstuffs which they consume. With all their factories and work-shops in successful operation, the proportion of home-grown cereals would be still smaller. Every increase in the manufacturing prosperity of the east creates a larger demand for western products. The facilities for exchange ought to correspond with the rapidly expanding needs of commerce. Public works which are universal in their benefits should be built at the national cost; therefore our Government, in the exercise of its sovereign right to regulate commerce, ought to undertake these internal improvements, and directly remove the impediments which now obstruct our inland navigation.

The boundless wealth of the present harvest will do much to restore our golden guide, bring back the American people to their earlier habit of prudent dealing, and re-establish business on a basis of stable values. In 1860, the Agricultural Bureau, judging from the growth of previous years, estimated the total grain crop of the Mississippi valley for the year 1880 at 1,200,000,000 bushels. In 1874, the product was already 1,455,000,000 bushels; and in 1877, the aggregate must approach 1,950,000,000 bushels, which was the estimated yield of 1890. So greatly does the rapidity of our development outstrip calculation. Our tillage will fill our tills. The golden harvest of 1877 will relieve the financial embarrassments of the country and re-establish business on a sound basis.

The currency of the Mississippi is gold-bearing. The profits arising from the general revival of trade which the shipments of our crops would cause would far exceed the outlays required for the improvement of the river. The imperial stream which is able to play so important a part in the movement of these harvests and in the restoration of public prosperity ought at once to be put into a state of efficient usefulness.

INTERESTS OF AMERICAN SHIPPING.

During the civil war, our commercial marine was swept from the ocean. Thousands of sailors have been driven from lucrative employment, and our country has lost the rich profits of the carrying-trade and the ready means of defense which spring from this training-school of marines. The present moment seems to be favorable for the United States to regain its maritime ascendency. *American* vessels ought to convey the cargoes and secure the profits of our foreign commerce.

The practical success of the jetties seems now to be an established fact.* By their action, the sand-bar at the mouth of the South Pass has been removed, and now Atlantic steamers drawing twenty-two feet of water can sail without obstruction to the wharves of New Orleans. With a deepened channel, the Mississippi would bear abundant freights to the ocean steamships, and greatly aid the Government in its efforts to retrieve our marine prosperity. Deduct from our foreign trade the commodities which are now borne to the sea-board by the Mississippi river, and the total is materially lessened. But the present traffic is inconsiderable in comparison with the possibilities of our river commerce. In 1876, more than 190,000,000 bushels of cereals were received at the ports of Portland, Boston, New York, Philadelphia and Baltimore; and of this quantity over 100,000,000 bushels were shipped to foreign

* The United States Inspector, whose duty it is to report to the Government the progress of the work and the depth of the channel, has officially notified the Secretary of War that on the 22d of December there was a practicable channel through the jetties two hundred feet wide and twenty-three and a half feet deep at average flood-tide. There is every probability that the natural forces now operating under the control of the jetties will soon dredge a channel thirty feet deep through the bar at the mouth of the Mississippi.

lands. It is true that some of this grain is grown too far north or east to be carried to market by the Mississippi, but take all the breadstuffs, all the other crops of the farm, all the products of the mill and the work-shop, which from the adjacency of the places of growth or manufacture are naturally tributary to the river trade, and the whole amount of merchandise which might be conveyed to the sea-board by the Mississippi would swell our foreign commerce to vast proportions. The beneficial effect which the river-borne cargoes of this valley would exert upon the interests of American shipping is still another powerful argument in favor of the improvement of the Mississippi river.

INCREASED DEMAND FOR AMERICAN BREADSTUFFS.

Russia is the greatest wheat-producing country in Europe. Jealous of his military fame, the Czar will never consent to peace under the humiliation of defeat. The numerous reverses of the Russian arms—though retrieved by late successes—render it probable that hostilities will continue through another campaign. Meanwhile the tumults of war will unsettle agricultural industry in southern Russia, and the need of fresh levies will withdraw the tillers of the soil from productive labor. During the coming season, Russia will scarcely be able to export grain to meet the requirements of the rest of Europe. The continuance of the famine in the Madras and Bengal presidencies will diminish the exportation of wheat from India, while the partial failure of the grain crops in Europe and the wants of contending armies will probably create an unusually large demand for American breadstuffs. But there is no need of prediction, for the enlarged demand is already a recorded fact.

Recently published tables of British imports show that the importation of wheat during the first eight months of the present year *exceeded* the receipts for the corresponding months of 1876 by $20,000,000!

Out of 80,000,000 bushels of breadstuffs imported into England during the current year up to August 31st, 60,000,000 bushels were shipped from the United States. During the eight weeks preceding October 17th, the export of wheat from this country was over 8,500,000 bushels more than our shipments for the corresponding period of last year.

SAFETY OF THE GULF ROUTE.

The earlier apprehension that grain exported by the Mississippi route would be injured by the climate of the Gulf has been dissipated by commercial experience. During all the years of shipment by river, the cases of damage have been so very rare as to prove that any fear of injury by the moisture or temperature of the Gulf is substantially baseless. For many years, California, Russia and India have been carrying on a large and increasing grain-trade with Europe. With infrequent exceptions, the freights have arrived uninjured. But the wheat exported from California twice traverses tropical waters; the cereals from Odessa encounter the sultry climate of the Mediterranean; and the Indian grain consigned to English markets is exposed to the torrid temperature of the Arabian and Red Seas. If cargoes subjected for a longer time to intenser heat reach their destination in safety, no climatic objection to the Gulf route can be valid.

EXAMPLE OF THE UNITED KINGDOM.

Great Britain has maintained its marvelous commercial sovereignty by the enterprise of its citizens and the wisdom of its legislation. It has fostered its trade by protective laws and vast systems of marine and internal improvements.

These public works not only facilitate the operations of commerce, but they also bind together the empire with the indissoluble ties of material interest, and furnish the nation with a rapid means of military concentration and defense. In its patronage of internal improvements, the example of England is well worthy of American imitation. Our Government ought to exercise the forecast and provide the facilities which will win and preserve mercantile supremacy.

REASONS FOR IMMEDIATE ACTION.

The times are specially favorable for the construction of public works. Labor is cheap, and tens of thousands of workingmen are out of employment. Clearly it is not the duty of the Government to provide occupation for men whom a depression of business has thrown out of place; but, if the improvements are necessary and can now be made with unusual economy, it certainly is a strong argument in favor of the undertaking, that a present prosecution of the work would bring relief to many needy families, and measurably hasten the return of our disordered industries to a healthful condition.

The special methods of improvement may safely be left to science. With an adequate supply of means, civil engineering, using the disciplined forces of nature, can now make an easy conquest of physical obstacles. Assuredly the skill which abroad has excavated a strait between oceans and pierced mountain ranges with the avenues of commerce, and which at home has opened Hurl Gate, built the jetties, and dug the Keokuk canal, is equal to the task of removing sand-bars. Even in the dryest seasons, there is always enough water in the Mississippi for the service of commerce, but its diffusion over so broad a bed causes obstructive shallows. The stream must be deepened by contraction within narrower limits, and compelled to exert its mighty energies to dredge out its own channel; or else the available lakes of Minnesota must be used as reservoirs to supply a full tide during the season of low water.

In times past, an occasional extravagance in expenditure, or imperfection in the structures, has aroused popular prejudice against the whole system, and temporarily defeated improvements essential to the commercial convenience of the nation.

The most rigorous economy and thoroughly effective work will alone entitle such undertakings to the present favor of Congress.

An active co-operation of allied interests, forgetful of minor issues, persistent in effort, and jealous only of divisions which would defeat the common hope, would surely command success.

And then the Mississippi river—whose southward course was divinely directed, in order that it might, by facilitating the exchanges of different climes, more completely subserve the wants of man—would fulfil its grand and natural functions in the commerce of the world.

In the hope that the action of this Convention may result in an early accomplishment of the desired object, I am,

> Respectfully, yours,
>
> SYLVESTER WATERHOUSE.

www.ingramcontent.com/pod-product-compliance
Lightning Source LLC
Chambersburg PA
CBHW032141080426
42733CB00008B/1157